Illustrious
for Brief Moments

poems by

Renee Podunovich

Finishing Line Press
Georgetown, Kentucky

Illustrious for Brief Moments

Copyright © 2021 by Renee Podunovich
ISBN 978-1-64662-427-0 First Edition
All rights reserved under International and Pan-American Copyright Conventions. No part of this book may be reproduced in any manner whatsoever without written permission from the publisher, except in the case of brief quotations embodied in critical articles and reviews.

ACKNOWLEDGMENTS

"Allowing", *The Mindful Word*, 2018 https://www.themindfulword.org/2018/soulful-poems-renee-podunovich/ This poem will also be on permanent display as part of the Ridgeway Alley Poems Project in Ridgeway, CO.
"Another Season", *SW Colorado Arts Perspective Magazine*, 2013 https://issuu.com/artsperspective/docs/apissue33_sport_final-web
"Darkening", *The Mindful Word*, 2018 https://www.themindfulword.org/2018/soulful-poems-renee-podunovich/
"Illustrious for Brief Moments", *Journey of the Heart: Women's Spiritual Poetry Blog*, 2020 https://womenspiritualpoetry.blogspot.com/2020/11/illustrious-for-brief-moments-by-renee.html
"Reverie", *Journey of the Heart: Women's Spiritual Poetry Blog*, 2019 https://womenspiritualpoetry.blogspot.com/2019/01/reverie-by-renee-podunvich.
"The Poet's Broken Heart", Winner 2019 Cantor Award, *Telluride Institute Online*, 2019 https://www.tellurideinstitute.org/wp-content/uploads/2019/06/Y-PodunovichThePoets19-renee-podunovich.pdf
"The Sea and the Unseen", 2018 https://www.themindfulword.org/2018/soulful-poems-renee-podunovich/
"Witnessed", 2018 https://www.themindfulword.org/2018/soulful-poems-renee-podunovich/

Publisher: Leah Huete de Maines
Editor: Christen Kincaid
Cover Art: "*We are of Pleiades*, 6 of 7" by Sonja Horoshko, 1991, acrylic on canvas www.SonjaHoroshko.com
Author Photo: Aspen Russo, Aspen Jade Photography
Cover Design: Elizabeth Maines McCleavy

Order online: www.finishinglinepress.com
also available on amazon.com

Author inquiries and mail orders:
Finishing Line Press
PO Box 1626
Georgetown, Kentucky 40324
USA

Table of Contents

Allowing 1

The Poet's Broken Heart 2

Moon Lace 4

Darkening 5

Reverie 6

Dream Rain 7

The Hidden Largest 8

Dolores River of Sorrows 9

Witnessed 10

Sparrow 11

Illustrious for Brief Moments 12

Icicle Medicine 13

Wind Triptych: How She Awakens You 15

Feeding Blossoms to the River 17

Dreaming to Waking Dreams 19

Bright Sleep 20

Another Season 21

Summer Lunacy 22

The Poet's Bouquet 23

Shelter 24

Skeleton River 26

Clear View 27

Waking from Ever-Winter 28

Down River 30

Canyon Time 32

Dining With My Muse 33

The Sea and The Unseen 35

Additional Acknowledgments 36

Allowing

There was no way to clear
this ancient oak grove
without adding
one more grief to the world.

So just let Her be this
wild and tangled and uncertain.

All of the leaves are on the branches
or have fallen to soil,
except the one
pressed on this page of my journal.

The Poet's Broken Heart

"Your heart is like an aperture,"
says the confident clinician I have hired
to help me make sense out of my pain.

I consider this as I stare
        at the charred heartmeat
I have unpacked from a wicker picnic basket,
presented on a delicate china plate,
an embroidered linen napkin folded neatly in my lap,
heavy silver utensils in hand,
        in preparation for cannibalizing
        my own demise.

"One can learn to open it to varying degrees," she claims,
"You can close it to protect yourself."
I imagine how things might have been different
if I had known this
        before I took this once beating organ
        and proceeded to gradually filet it,
        throw it willingly on a grill,
        but not just any grill—
the most cryptic and deceptive one,
the one most likely to start out with mild heat,
the kind of heat like early summer sun on my bare shoulders,
that feel-good warmth that seems benevolent,
        inspires juices to drip onto coals,
        seductively stimulating them
so that I hardly noticed the fact that
I was burning.

Yet I never pulled back, even when the fat dripped,
flaming that intensity,
even when I realized that yes, I am choosing
        to be seared alive,
        have lost my preservation instinct—
the one rational people, like this therapist,
use to shelter their tenderness in the face of annihilation.

But not my poet's heart.
Instead, I opened the aperture all the way,
despite the blisters, the smell of feverish flesh,
let any discernment about safety
        disappear into flames.
And now I sit, this overcooked mess on a plate—
and the tears come, tears of disbelief,
that I can love so deeply;
not because I am a saint,
because this is what it takes
to prepare a poem in a wounded world like ours:

        I didn't open myself so wide
        only because I loved you.
        That part is irrelevant.

I did it for my own healing,
I was hunting for these words,
now tucked secretly inside me.
And at the end of the therapy hour,
I pack up this picnic of my undoing
and tonight when the moon is full,
        I will walk into the desert,
        find a certain place on red earth
        where the moonlight is lace and ethereal,
will nurse my own wounds,
take this overworked cardiac steak
in my bare hands,
lift it so that moonlight bites
and stars alight on scorched surfaces,
        and the words will pour forth from me,
        because by the sheer will of my art
        I will be raw again.

Moon Lace

High desert, autumn nights,
I sip stars and night swim
      with my mistress moon,
she dresses me in a gown of finely laced light,
spidery and buoyant, her enchantment is a snare
      —entangling.

She weaves me into her thin glimmers,
twisting a glow into the curls of my hair
that scatter like snaking vines along the ruby dirt,
my skin luminous satin, a smooth surface
for the embroidered frills and flounces
she laces upon my neck,
      delicate gossamers looped, plaited, knotted
      into a decorative and illusory noose.

I have imagined myself as a million beautiful
yet time-bound things.
In every bondage
is the key to breaking free—

escape is simple here in the desert
where the scale of the warp and weft
and the arid conditions render her ties brittle,
      releasing flowing flower motifs and artifices
      that snap and break
      in their exposure to vastness.

Darkening

I.
Put the light out,
go dark.
Retreat back to the humming earth,
her cloak opens to enfold you
as you will unfold your subtle body
into the filaments of the universe nocturnal.

II.
Rest your trauma-heart.
Let the Godmothers take care of these sufferings
while you burrow and dream,
        be a white rabbit so still
        only a quiver of whiskers reveals you, waiting
        to dart unrestricted into open spaces,
        through expansive meadow and yawning glade—

III.
But that is not yet.
Now is to repose, become invisible,
though not in a deficient, aching way.
        Be unseen in softness,
        the way a velvet scarf brushes
        along your soulskin, touched
by mystery so vast in its sentience
that all you can do is listen

IV.
and if you are diligent, you will catch one note
of cosmic music echoing like whale song
        with no words legible
        yet every cell recognizes
that sorrow, that longing for pod,
that joy in swimming

        full and large and unapologetic
        in the elements—
        free in the fleeting

Reverie
> *for Sonja*

she lives by herself and hunts, but she is not a stray cat. she is movement,
a nocturne, a blanket spread out in the park, a knife cutting apricots
and green chilies, a dish with a floral pattern, a textile draped over
furniture, rice paper and cerulean ink, silver and turquoise,
the rose and lime and umber stones that are the palette
of the desert landscape.
she is a bluebird on a juniper branch,
a bluebird printed on a cloth flour sack,
a Tibetan bell at the front door,
a brass bed frame used as a trellis in the garden,
a trail that is circular,
pots of pink geraniums beneath the sagebrush,
the black and white stripes of a sun umbrella,
chime-song in spring winds and
recumbent vines of morning glory radiant with dew.

beauty billows out in waves
from an introverted doorway of a delicate bungalow on an irregular
block, where she paints or writes by a wood stove,
serves gin with sprigs of garden mint in old-fashioned glasses,
splurges on blue cheese and gingersnaps,
keeps company with watercolors, black cats and pianos.

sometimes she is jet stones strung on wire with tears and pearls,
heavy like layers of Pendleton blankets stacked so high
their distinctive designs overlap then disappear in the night
and she sleeps and sleeps in the art of dreams—

> her bed is a web of stars
> where certain sadnesses barely make a dent
> in the enormous body of space and dark matter.

Dream Rain
    after Hurricane Rosa, 2018

I woke to the sound of her fingers
thrumming on the roof,
on my sternum—   her water hair
        each strand drizzling,
        skimming my face
        (only dreams)
she placed tears in my eye sockets,
they fell out of the corners,
    wet quartz tumbling
onto my pillow, evaporated
by morning   —absorbed back into her mist.

They say she is a feminine rain
when she is slow and steady,
so light in the falling that only gradually
    will the bark of Juniper become black,
    the once subdued needles now vibrant jade.

I slept in her ocean,
deep in the underwater rivers that form her waving.
I wake to a wet desert,
and her tears caught on spider webs and wires.
I lift a single raindrop, lay it on my third eye,
the place still concerned about an absolute sorrow,
    a permanent loss
I can do nothing to soothe.

If I successfully wrestle my darkness
each night, if her hands
occasionally caress me in shadows—
        the broken drought,
        the end of longing,
        a quenched healing
            that arrives only
            at its own tempo.

The Hidden Largest

The largest mountain range is under the Atlantic Ocean.
It forms one arm connected to oceanic ridges
in every ocean, creating the longest mountain range in the world,
the deepest canyons, the cause of Pangaea —
    80 million years
continents still drifting, friction, unstable, plate tectonics,
propagating velocities, seismic migration.

Portions with enough elevation extend above the sea.
To navigate these, use a bearing compass, a nautical almanac
and align with the magnetic poles and the stars.
Know that surface water bulges outward and inward,
mimicking the rough terrain below
(but this is too small to be seen without measuring the altitude
above the water from a satellite).
Forget your eyes altogether: The mind can't swim.

Discard the logical tools for observing surfaces.
As ocean levels rise, as land slips beneath,
and what was solid dissolves,
learn to trace voice and movement —
    how the heavy sound of your tears and longings,
    and the buoyant notes of your love songs
all bounce easily off the edges of the world submerged,
returning and reverberating, measuring the distance between self
    and the connection to everything else.

Below what the eye can automatically define are immense spaces;
where the aquatic heart, the untamed self,
and everything truly substantial
    dance weightless
    underwater.

Dolores, River of Sorrows

In the time of Raven Dark
let no light shine
so that the black balm
of curling invisible
heals you where the hurt fell.

There is a tear in her heart
       for your suffering.
Catch it in your palm
so that your hand harms no more,
close your fist around this liquid compassion—
no rage can crush healing water.

Grief released is the river's flow,
she will be merciful when you whisper
your songs of brokenness
into her eddies and tides,
       suddenly one morning, emotional freedom
       like a vapor
       will swill and churn in a rush
       of spring thaw.

Witnessed

a healing story unfolds like
the inner curve of shell,
lined with a smoothness
that comes from allowing
the heart to be observed
      vulnerable,
        the risk of contact,
        the bind of shame,
        the need to be seen
and the push away from need.

a dry river stone narrative
cautiously quarried from exile,
      once recognized and considered
      is a dull grey weight in the hand.

now, submerged in the gaze of another
or in water-under-ice-flowing-yet-in-winter,
unexpected hidden colors are revealed—
      sage, umber, amethyst, gold,
      hues that fold fragments of self
back into an abiding
unbound
whole

tender in the mending

Sparrow

Black and delicate,
I let you loose onto a current of crimson wind,
unsure how well you will fly—
    I know you will.
You somehow landed in my lap
for just a minute in the immensity of time,
just long enough for me to wonder
how you became so broken,
long enough that my heart would open
to your dark feathers and sorrowful songs,
and my own veiled wounds,
exposed to me again.

I imagine the time I stroked your soft head,
the feathers there tender and downy—
    just for that instant, you were loved completely;
    you let go of the need to harm yourself
    and considered your own beauty instead.

The second before I let you go,
I became a window, panes of glass
transparent and unafraid to open fully.
I have closed the shutters now,
can no longer track your flight.
Where you journey,
    it isn't for me to know.
You were not mine to keep,
were mine only for that brief moment:
a fragment of a dream,
one note of interstellar song:

    the impression you left—
    a thousand times the actual weight
    of your light, hollow bones.

Illustrious for Brief Moments

Today is another chance
    to be fully alive,
    present in the What
        Is—   the light and dark embodied,
                      the movement from dreaming
                      to waking dreams—all of it
                      the same mysterious fabric.

Sunrise—Juncos feast at the feeder
cheerful in the chill white,
light lands on feathers and drifts,
                on me at my writing desk,
                on you, somewhere—

                Webs of distance
I won't write about longing ever again.
I have already wandered that endless path,
followed it to the distant most planets.

I am here, not there, not anywhere else.
I exist inside the silk lining
        of pockets of snow, softly
elevating me and the winter birds
far far from our summer selves,
                stillness, seeds and scattered
                words become our

                dream food.

We are held aloft—illustrious—for brief moments
before our feet sink through
to the solid, frozen earth,
dark matter, the underworld
                that will once again
                birth us at
                sunrise—

Icicle Medicine

I.
She is first a fine snow—
the space between the snowflakes,
the cosmos between the notes in *Für Alina*,
the emptiness inside the complexity of fractals.

Call her cold love to you, let her chill
slide its hands along your spine,
she hunts your warmth, to melt her,
      return her to a river she once was.

Rippling free with summer rain,
soft and dancerly she flowed,
and you remind her of what she will be again
in spring: rapid, lush, and reckless.

II.
Everywhere you go,
she is in your cells,
she is your mistress:
the one you sing praises to at dawn,

the one you enter at night,
naked and submissive to her faithful movements,
letting moon song and dragonflies
swim with your soul whisperings.

Put your ear to her icy current
and she tells you what is true,
      about your own confused heart.

III.
She takes illusions and freezes them,
each flake a frozen fantasy, a particular
pattern reflecting your wholeness

—what is healed
and the lingering wounds—

the love and the shadows,
they fall around you this early morning in January,
       after the moon was cloaked,
       and it was just your unwinding
       and the spiraling stars all night.

This is your gift—
to be holographic,
to hover in the interstitial knowing,
the whole purpose of an icicle
       is to clarify what is fixed,
       a shimmering, frozen dream.

Wind Triptych: How She Awakens You

I.
For so long now, her airy body
was saturated with water,
adorned with moisture and unpredictability:
holding space for what needed to be sung
        in tones of wet and hues of blue all winter.
In the endless opaque nights—
you were entangled in a sleepy dream net,
in dark imaginings, still swimming the invisible.

Suddenly early spring, and she is simply wind.
Be certain: she will not spare you.
You will not be left to linger, dreaming
yet of frozen stillness and arctic rest.
She jabs you awake, fingers like thistles and gusts,
pulling away the imaginal filigrees
that tangled around your limbs like moonflowers,
just illusions, blown into the surety of impermanence.

She is how things move through vastness,
        over eternities and infinities;
nothing and no one can hide
from her ambition to heal and transform.
She awakens you from inertia
and there is nothing to do
but let her have her way with you.

II.
Bracing against her turbulence is to remain stagnant,
a stubborn icicle unwilling to melt, refusing to fall
into the embrace of the barely thawed river,
that beckoning spillway of snow disguising
the coldest water imaginable—
        imagine how it will shock you
        once you find the courage to let go.

Turning your back on her flighty chants
is retrograde, a default to familiar landscapes
— the terrain of your wounding
and your addiction to the wounds—

Stand and face her, in all of her intensity,
if you flinch at her ferocity,
you will miss the gentle caresses,
the touch that finally melts you,
frees you from years of aching,
held within your need for holding.

III.
Stretch out your curled up body
inside the basket of her tempest,
unafraid of the sound of her wailing
as she flies unencumbered over sagebrush and irises—
become the spores and pollens
carried to unknown lands, taking hold on new ground,
let the husks of what you are no longer
peel away by her force,
uncovering a tender skin, you thought you had lost.

Your new skin tingles
under her feather breath—
she gathers the years of grief,
spins that suffering into a cyclone or spiral,
flinging it to the edges of this atmosphere
or maybe into the arms of the furthest cosmic storms:

And you land deep
inside the fresh territory of possibility
and your own ground calling you home.

Feeding Blossoms to the River

Clouds
and shadows of clouds on rims exposed,
    not black and white,
not that defined: clarity is for fools,
not for pale, flowering plums—
    who realize it could still freeze
    any night now.

Things always work out, I was always told.
Sometimes they don't:
    this plum tree in all its yearning,
    the passionate pink of its super bloom,
    could be met with a knife of ice,
and while the flooding of the river is checked
by continued cool nights and barely warming days,
the tenderhearted, who show their delicacy freely,
suffer in a world of ever-extremes
and unpredictable forces.

I keep finding ways to turn disappointments
    into cherry blossoms, have felt I must.
This time, I broke open far too wide,
past the point of ever retracting
to the simple safety of a bud.
    If I die of exposure—c'est la vie!
And if my beautiful plum petals
should meet that freeze,
I will wake tomorrow to see them
wet and faded, their refinement and cadence
    now brown and wilting.

No matter what, I will, myself, take handfuls
    of living or dead flowers to the river
      (though I can't stand to lose one more thing)
will offer their tenderness
to the imminent flood—her rush
is another lesson:
      that nothing exists outside the flowing
      uncertainty of this life.

She carries in her fullness
the things ready to be uprooted and washed away,
empty space in the banks fills with wet mud,
leaving a blank canvas.
Grief doesn't care what takes hold there,
has no expectations,
just listens to the wordlessness
of her audacious water, brown and choppy,
momentum a magic inside her liquid muscles,
her waves slap at my feet,
sharp the ice-cold stings skin,
sun warms stone where I ruminate,
    witnessing change,
    attempting to be the unknown,
    rather than afraid of it.

Dreaming to Waking Dreams

morning is fresh wind in bones, monsoons,
a hope that gestated all night: to feel ease,
easy all summer, eating flowers
for breakfast, becoming their colors
in the sunshine, skin
like peacock feathers, prismatic, dressed
to enter the pageantry of being awake

>night eyes—weighty emeralds that finally close,
>receive instruction on how to arrange letters
>made of electricity and silk threads
>in a geometric pattern only understood in sleep

waking again (endless) all of it gone,
disappearance of those night lands,
enchanted nocturnal wilderness
that daily commotion eclipses

>all day long—business,
>aware that I left many soul tasks
>undone in the dreamtime.
>In daylight I am a sunflower,
>must follow that solar gaze
>all the way to its descent in the far west—

then darkness (released) slip
into mysteries, freedom within ever-
unfolding, belong in the shadows,
lightless flight, the dream-maker is my
courtesan, let her take me dancing, follow
her lead, fluently, limber, willing
to let go, my daytime costume
unbuttoned, persona undone—

>exposing my nocturnal essence,
>a perfume of self
>unbound: saline, willow bark, roses,
>top notes of lemon and still, surprisingly
>tears...

Bright Sleep

Sheer silk rays of light wrap around my figure,
lunar hands hold my belly and thighs,
moon sighs, a cobalt slumber of soul rest,
the caress of moon lips over cheeks,
planting wet kisses on wrists, fits
      of tossing and turning, churning
          the day's activity into dream language.

Every morning my mouth tries to shape words
from those nocturnal symbols,
but the solace of that illuminated crescent
      has faded with the rising sun.
If she exists in the daytime it is only as powder,
not as her shadow radiance simmered
in space waters, vast teapot of the galaxy,
brilliant and sure, pouring a most fantastic liquid
      into my night visions,
         collision of self with enormity—

I become a single finger of moonbeam
reaching out for my own heart
as it rests in my sleeping body:
      a symbol tucked
         inside the cosmic dream.

Another Season

all winter, deep underground,
root fingers have sensed
the way into the dark:
>how eyes fail in lack of light,
>that dark tumble, finding openings,
>pushing further, minute motion,
>friction and ease.

in the heat of another season
her body is certainly a peony in full bloom—
luminous and intricate, the scent of infinity
seeps through petals, sifting
into summer sunshine.

if you try to distill that essence,
>it will elude you.
you must slowly stalk that outrageous flower.
don't try to grab her
with your hands of flesh and hard bone
skeleton. stay supple, surprised by her serenity
and the sigh of her movement
under ferocious spring winds.

you must softly whisper, "Beautiful."
"May I?"
>"I must."
Her longing will brush the tip of your nose,
her scent will haunt you.
she sways on the thinnest stem,
ecstatic under your gaze,
under the weight of her own
>existence
and the anticipation of
silk moon kisses
tonight.

Summer Lunacy

Spinning out into sunshine
the way it pulls us all toward
its glowing, heat, desire
on skin, sweat, buzzing
insects, cricket hum, songs of self
unsleeping, the outermost expression
of all that was imagined in dream ice.

I sway with the delight of sap,
pollen, swollen motion of wind
in petals, the land lush beneath
bare feet. I am open,
I am going mad, losing grip
on what I thought I was,
letting myself disrobe, that old skin—
      the one I didn't choose,
      I wore it to survive,
      a covering that no longer serves me.

Valerian flowers, unadorned, praise the sliver of moon,
that goddess, crescent and disappearing,
stripping off the lacy slip of shine
she wore all month, now
she is unknown, even to herself,
there is no establishing dominance
or control over her hidden countenance.

Dark moon: kneel before her
      —empty—
inside the panicked heart, she rubs
her chaos into my fear,
a balm that finally soothes
      the not knowing,
      the beyond logic,
      the trying not to see
      anything but that darkness,
giving way to senses unbound, swirl stars,
hushed breath, glimmer deep, liberated
in nectar of night and eclipsed light.

The Poet's Bouquet
    for Russ

I wake to Sego Lilies—
two stems of elegantly pale flowers
he picked for me in the field
        he was irrigating,
        setting water loose onto land,
        guiding its flow, letting it move
        to the places that thirst the most.

He knows how to handle precious things:
with care, caressed, soothed, the lightest touch,
steady, invited, never forced or coerced.
Last night, he took my hand,
showed me how he had placed them
in a blue glass on my writing desk.
        "They are closed tonight," he said,
        holding me next to his warmth
        under the Strawberry Full Moon.
        He assures me, "They will open again tomorrow."

Every morning, I write poems to heal fragments,
and the lilies open their subtle bodies as dawn ripens.
With him, it is always safe to open—
        his heart is the core of these blossoms,
        the yellow and amethyst,
        the sepal and stamens.
        I fall in, again and again,
        to the perfection of this design,
        into a love that invites me
        toward my own healed center.

This is how he loves me:
        Sego Lilies offered to my heartwords

Shelter
> *at Mesa Verde National Park*

I don't know if I know
how to listen to silences so old,
quietude contained within rock
crafted into brick, held in a mortar
of mud and pebbles, bound
in ancient spring water and clay.

    Minds speculate:
what must have been, what still is,
the living traditions we struggle to maintain,
how we find and lose meaning,
place and displace our humanness,
forget our belonging on the earth, strive
then and now to survive.

Thunder in the cradle of the canyon.
A few drops of rain land on my cheeks
and on high desert dust.
    I let cool wind brush my hair, caress my brow,
    let my head rest in the laps of ancient women
who made comfort out of a landscape,
out of their call to nurture life.
I don't want to know
anything but this stillness,
this moment away from the entire world,
    this gap in time.

I could settle here, let exhausted bones
and my burning, broken-down heart
relax into stasis
next to grinding stones
unused now for hundreds of years—
they offer just the hint of the effort it takes
to be well and thrive in this life,
    to bear witness to change,
    to know ends will come,
    stopping points.

Invisibility invites each one of us
into its grace, as graceful
as alcoves of stone in rainstorms,
inside the shelter of awe.

Skeleton River

Fall heart, see-through wet.
Let go. Grief is crimson silt—
blue stones invite rest.

River low, exposed
asleep stones, silt now settles
in spaces between.

Silt just memory,
hue of river red in spring,
all that coursed: ending.

Clear View

Iceblue before sun crests,
just a few flickers of saffron sail
over the horizon line,
possibility—

    hush, wait in the quiet
    for that luminosity, that moment
when light finally lands on the winter fields;
grasses bent, the weight of snowflakes,
frost fringes their honeyed stalks, shimmers,
shivers, swims in snowbanks, sun-splashed.

I place myself in the center of my life once again,
will let this warmth cover me too.
I belong here, in the middle, centripetal
and still I dance

    with you, we are bright
    like embers, like night stars
    sparkling the black universe,
    our hearts on fire, ablaze
    with elation, vibrantly
    unburdened from all
    that was let go.

I burned everything
that blocked my clear view.
Now, ash and fallow make space,
an invitation, an opening.

Something new will grow here,
and I intend to tend it well.

Waking from Ever-Winter
at Butler Wash, UT

I.

Wetfrozen silver leaves,
the cottonwoods let them fall,
    their bodies now a pattern—
    grey decay against ochre sand,
    a trail lined with death
    even as we live and walk and breathe.

Vapors of desert snow,
mist from a storm now past,
in sunny spots ice gives way
to transparent pools of that melted chill.
    I look for signs of life, movement
    in water's depths, and even though I know
    there is nothing yet to find,
I can't stop wanting that wordless thing,
how I long for something I can't quite name—

the lasting, timeless, beckoning call inside
bodycells, the dreambody, our ceaselessness
through deep time, dimensions, and multiverses.

II.

Hibernation still calls to my bones,
even as my blood runs fire.
Despite the sway of cross-quarter quickening,
the full moon is a stronger sedative,
    lulls me back to sleep,
    an ever-winter slumber.

It takes all of the seasons for the heart to mend,
for new awareness to find hold,
and what is next is just a seed dreaming
in the still frozen ground of February.

I settle myself back in, invite that vision to find me—

    I am quiet, still, receptive,
    lustrous like these small pools;
    vessels inside a canyon spillway.

III.

Rivers I cried, they flooded this sandstone wash,
scarlet dirt hewn by that outpouring,
earth polished so fine it is impossible to capture,
    the tiniest, smoothest gemstones,
    cherry and glistening in the light,
    falling through my fingers like an hourglass—

this is how it is to fade: appearances gone,
just the bare facts are left; they are hard to perceive,
like staring into the sun on a winter day:
    we live and disappear; we are only ourselves.

IV.

Ancient frogs painted yellowred on stone
snap me awake, suddenly,
they steal my breath away, they chant
their long ago song; it's my own heartbeat
    pounding my ears, then wind, then stillness.

I let the ice deliver its cold smart to my fingers,
I let myself be affected again—I won't hide from living—

I will walk alone or with another,
I will sing more songs and I will not sing,
I am going to dance when the moon is dark,
I am still falling apart but something whole is emerging,
    the way water invites everything to be near it.
    I drink my fill, then offer some to the world.

I am mystified by simplicity;
there is nothing to be other than my next inhale.

Down River
> *at the Lower Dolores*

On the silver feathered backbone
      of an exhale—
         watch grief fly
free as swallows skimming winter waters,
soaring on gales of transience.
Your sorrows released evaporate,
vanish into slickrock, into the mouth
of this river-carved canyon.
         Never ask for them back.

Gather soul medicines found along the path:
rose hips, sage, cedar, and lichen
sodden from last night's snow,
their colors momentarily radiant
under melting crystals of frost.
      —Inhale:
the vanilla scent of pinion pitch,
a resin that seals the heart,
covers the fissures, restores your tenderness.

Only a scar remains, only noticeable when stars fall,
trails of light across the midnight psyche,
a remnant ache you will keep—
        your own darkness harnessed.
You have learned to wander that precarious edge,
where the conscious and Unconscious meet;
using your subtle body, a place deeper than logic,
and out of obscurity you have scavenged
        a more durable self,
extracted from galaxies and mystery
with the sharp tip of a crescent moon.

Each new year (or day or minute) is an opening,
an opportunity to be bright like river ripples,
sunlit and willingly carried,
held and pushed forward at the same time;
in every moment all facets are happening.
   —Be vast enough—
stretch to contain a dash more sparkle and night.
There is time yet for more,
a day or many; it is unclear
         but we are alive still in air, in water, the fire body,
         in each grateful breath.

Canyon Time
>*at Yellow Jacket Canyon*

Radiance on ridges reveals timespans,
stacked strata of landscape
traversed to the Middle Jurrasic layer,
>where phenomena from 150 million years ago
>created a jagged sandstone ledge,
>and here you find a welcoming spot for tea.

Wind and water-carved basins
hold a tablespoon or a cup of dirt,
just enough that in spring
tenacious seeds took dubious hold,
charmed by dewdrops and erratic rains,
>and now your teatime is wreathed
>with high desert wildflowers,
>each blossom cheerful and gold
>despite the probability that any day

a deluge will dislodge all efforts at permanence.

We forever tumble to new ground,
navigate constant shifts in terrain:
>the path of least resistance is down,
>seeking depth also creates height,
>the bottom is only momentary
>>or lasts millions of years,
>but the excavation is endless—
>>we are always exposed anew.

The most intimate layers of canyon and self—
gathering heat in the day, and at night
submerged under a cold ocean of stars,
>the planet spins and gravity embraces

our constant falling apart and resettlement.

Today, between these small and large movements,
sip your tea in a rare stillness,
find your essential center,
>the one known only inside the pause
>amidst Earth's ever-dances—

so gracefully we are carried
on stone through the galaxy.

Dining With My Muse

My muse—her sparkling charm,
she is all kinds of beauty
    and also a dark enchantress who savors pain
    served as a seven-course meal.
She crafts homebrews out of betrayals,
bakes disappointment into chocolate lava cakes,
serves them with not a thought
of how they might make her dinner guests weep
as they remember their own deepest wounds;
    the ones shoved into lightless corners,
    where cobwebs and dust motes reside.

She spends days, weeks, years
gathering the terrible ingredients for these poetic feasts.
Life always delivers the components she needs,
especially when she is not paying attention;
that is when the most difficult things appear in her larder:
    unexpected, out of the blue, from left of center,
    hit by a meteor, blind-sided ingredients.

Oh, my muse! She loves a candid meal;
one that wasn't in the Joy of Cooking,
that even Julia Childs would struggle to prepare.
There is a thrill in chaos, the reminder that life is
    mysterious, out of the ordinary,
and even if the menu was formulated from exquisite despair,
she knows she will make it into something palatable:
    a lavender shortbread cookie infused with heartbreak,
    a hearty winter stew in a broth of suffering,
    a white layer cake with strawberry filling,
    iced with loneliness and isolation.

If you sit at her table, my muse will lure you
into dining with her, will assure you
that consuming a meal of such depth and authenticity
is good for you. She will serve aperitif drinks;

Campari with soda and crocodile tears,
    so that you will relax into the next courses.
How could you say no to summer greens
topped with fresh apricots and your lost loves?
Or to cherries soaked in bourbon
    and that pit in your stomach dread?

If you dine with her until the last course,
you will be full and yet lighter somehow.
Her dishes are heavy yet leave you surprisingly refreshed.
She will offer strong coffee,
    topped with whipped cream,
        a dash of cardamom and honeysuckle syrup,
    and of course, a shot of innocence lost.

You won't be the same after dining with her.

The Sea and The Unseen
    at Salt Spring Island, BC

The smell of salt air will heal the ache in your soul.
The whales will sing your bones alive again.
You will leave behind the person you thought you were—
the scared one wrapped in a familiar scarf of smallness,
    as you step into the mystery of the dreamtime,
    in the powerful company of sisters.

You will return with joy like a Raven Iridescent
fluttering in your heart,
soaring within the spaciousness
that appears by caring for your own suffering,
    by tending to your own deep wounds.

You will carry home a basket of shells, songs and images
washed up from the depths of the Great Mother Sea—
    she will carry you back to the ones you love,
    and always, patiently, she awaits your return.

Additional Acknowledgments

Versions of Illustrious for Brief Moments, Bright Sleep, Moon Lace, Icicle Medicine, Dolores River of Sorrows, The Poet's Bouquet, Dream Rain and Skeleton River were printed at Mancos Common Press, 2019-2020. These are limited edition artist prints in collaboration with visual artist Sonja Horoshko.

Each poem was handset in 24pt Bookman Condensed lead type font by the poet, paired with a linocut print by the visual artist. 10 prints of each poem/image were made on a historic platen press using 100% rag archival paper. Six hand-bound manuscripts of the entire series titled "Paper Wings" were created by Podunovich and Horoshko during a collaborative artist residency at Willowtail Springs Nature Preserve in February of 2020 and have been published by the author and artist under Mancos Common Press. Inquire with author about purchase: www.ReneePodunovichPoet.com. Visit the Paper Wings blog: https://paperwingsletterpress.blogspot.com

www.ingramcontent.com/pod-product-compliance
Lightning Source LLC
LaVergne TN
LVHW041555070426
835507LV00011B/1097